BLACK PEARLS

Servants in the Households of the Báb and Bahá'u'lláh

SECOND EDITION

Bahá'í World Centre

THE INNER COURTYARD
of the house of the Tha Báb in Shiraz, now destroyed

BLACK PEARLS

Servants in the Households of the Báb and Bahá'u'lláh

SECOND EDITION

by
Abu'l-Qasim Afnan

KALIMÁT PRESS
LOS ANGELES

Library of Congress Cataloguing in Publication Data

Afnan, Abu'l-Qasim.
Black Pearls : servants in the household of the Báb and Bahá'u'lláh / by Abu'l-Qasim Afnan. -- 2nd ed.
p. cm.
Includes bibliographical references and index.
1. Slaves–Iran–Biography. 2. Blacks–Iran Biography. 3. Slavery and Islam–History. I. Title.
HT1286.A75 1999 305.5'67'092255--dc21 [B]
99-27903 CIP
ISBN 1-890688-03-7

Kalimát Press
1600 Sawtelle Boulevard, Suite 34,
Los Angeles, California 90025

www.kalimat.com

Cover design by Judy Liggett

To
Hand of the Cause of God,
ENOCH OLINGA,
the Father of Victories

CONTENTS

FOREWORD

to the Second Edition

FEW HISTORICAL INSTITUTIONS are more repugnant to our modern sensibilities than is chattel slavery. Other forms of human injustice and oppression continue to flourish, of course. But, the right of one human being to own another as property, once recognized by every nation in the world, is now universally repudiated and outlawed.

Nowhere is this feeling of repugnance for slavery stronger than in the United States, where slavery is associated–in a way that it is nowhere else–with racist theories and ideas of superiority of white over black. Africans were brought as slaves to the New World within a few years of Columbus's discovery. But they did not enter the

American colonies until 1619, more than one-hundred years later. Nonetheless, it was in North America that the most virulent notions of white supremacy were to take root and grow, bearing their bitter fruit in ways that we continue to experience today.

Certainly slavery was an ugly fact of life for centuries in the Caribbean, in Mexico, and in the Central and South American colonies of Spain and Portugal. Taken together, ten times as many Africans were transported to Latin America as were brought in chains to the United States. And they were brutally, inhumanly mistreated. Yet, racism never took hold in areas to the south in quite the same way as it did in the United States, for reasons that have never been adequately explained.

Despite our modern abhorrence, any student of history must realize that slavery as an institution was an accepted part of all human societies throughout most of history. It was only in the middle of the last century that it began to disappear. Before that, slavery was such a basic part of social life in most places that it was hardly even questioned. As such, it was sanctioned by both custom and religion.

The followers of Christ bought and sold slaves from the earliest days of Christianity. Certain passages in the Bible clearly approved the practice. Paul wrote:

> Slaves, be obedient to those who are your earthly masters, with fear and trembling, in singleness of heart, as to Christ . . . *

> Masters, treat your slaves justly and fairly, knowing that you also have a Master in heaven.**

These and other biblical passages were quoted often by Christian slave owners in America to justify the morality of their position, right up to the end of the Civil War.

Likewise, slavery was practiced in Muslim societies and deemed legal and acceptable by orthodox Muslims. The slave (*'abd*), especially the Muslim slave, had an accepted position in society. While certain passages in the Qur'an

* Ephesians 6:5
** Colossians 4:1

sought to improve the condition of slaves and encourage manumission, slavery was not outlawed and was implicitly sanctioned:

> And we have guided him to the two roads of
> Good and Evil.
> Yet he made no attempt to ascend the good.
> And what shall teach you about how to ascend?
> It is the freeing of a slave;
> Or feeding an orphan who is your kin,
> Or a poor man lying in the dust,
> In time of famine.*

The first and only world religion which insists on the prohibition of slavery in its Sacred Texts is the Bahá'í Faith. Slavery is here, for the first time, categorically and unambiguously forbidden to all believers. Bahá'u'lláh, in His famous epistle to Queen Victoria (1869), praised the British monarch for her efforts to abolish the slave trade:

> We have been informed that thou has forbidden the trading in slaves, both men and women. This, verily, is what God hath ordained in this wondrous Revelation. God hath, truly, destined a reward for thee, because of

* Qur'an 90:11-17

> this. He, verily, will pay the doer of good his due recompense . . .*

In His Most Holy Book, the Kitáb-i Aqdas (1873), Bahá'u'lláh has written:

> It is forbidden you to trade in slaves, be they men or women. It is not for him who is himself a servant to buy another of God's servants, and this hath been prohibited in His Holy Tablet. Thus, by His mercy, hath the commandment been recorded by the Pen of justice. Let no man exalt himself above another; all are but bondslaves before the Lord, and all exemplify the truth that there is none other God but Him.**

Thus, slavery is forbidden by Bahá'u'lláh on the grounds that it is incompatible with justice–the principle of the equality of all people before God, the oneness of humanity.

The enormous evil of slavery and the fact that it has now passed from civilized society should not, however, blind us to the history of those millions of men and women who lived their entire lives in bondage. Slaves were devalued by their

* *The Proclamation of Bahá'u'lláh* (Haifa: Bahá'í World Centre, 1967) pp. 33-34

** The Kitáb-i Aqdas, K72 (p. 45).

position in society–a position that Bahá'u'lláh has outlawed and rejected–but that does not mean that their lives were unimportant or that they have no story to tell.

Indeed, quite the opposite. Since we today believe that slavery was wrong, we should be eager to affirm in history the dignity and significance of the lives of individual slaves. We should hope to recover the stories, the sayings, the culture, and the biographies of slaves, in the same way that we would seek to reconstruct the personal histories of those whose stations in life were more fortunate. We should certainly guard against the danger of shifting the stigma of slavery onto the victims of the system, assuming that since bondage is distasteful so must be the lives and history of those who suffered under it.

Sadly, the latter view has most often prevailed. Because the lives of slaves–and of women, of the poor, and of others with low status in society –were accorded no value, their history has most often also been accorded no value as well–and so never recorded or deliberately forgotten. Such people are made invisible to history in this way, and it is easy for those who come after to conclude that they were unimportant, or perhaps did not exist at all.

For example, a survey of the many volumes that have been written on African-American history in the United States will show that little has been written about the individual lives of ordinary slaves. Even the history written by African Americans themselves tends to focus on the free, the rich, the powerful, and the famous–the "talented tenth," perhaps, of the black population who were, through heroic struggle, able to lift themselves above the rest and distinguish themselves with outstanding achievement. Or, the focus is on resistance and revolt, singling out those very few slaves (and others) who lashed out violently against the evil of their oppression. Serious attention given to the life of an ordinary slave is rare. Partially, of course, this is because information is sparse. But more seriously, it is because historians have pursued a path of "redemption" for black history–seeking to balance the horror of slavery with more positive images of African-American life.

But, to refuse to consider the life of the individual slave as a worthy subject for history implicitly rejects the idea that slaves claim a human dignity equal to their masters, and to all others. It inadvertently accepts the notion that slaves have no social value, that they were absent from history, and that they are objects unfit for study. We all must be proud of black heroes, of course, but we must not allow ourselves to forget those whose lives were not marked by extraordinary acts of defiance or outstanding achievement. This majority struggled against impossible odds to live their lives with dignity and purpose, and their lives are not without importance and meaning.

The writing of Bahá'í history has, of course, barely begun. In future decades and centuries, Bahá'í historians will no doubt fill whole libraries with the life stories of Bahá'í heroes and ordinary believers. The Bahá'í history books that we have today are mostly concerned with events associated with the Central Figures of the Faith and the lives of prominent believers. And, this is quite naturally so. Every Bahá'í will find deep meaning in *The Dawn-Breakers*, Nabil's chronicle of early Bábí history, or in *God Passes By*, Shoghi Effendi's summary of the first one-hundred years of Bahá'í history. But the brilliance of this early work should not blind us to the fact that there are also other stories to tell.

EDWARD G. BROWNE, in the early part of this century, lamented the lack of information about Táhirih found in Persian Bahá'í histories. Products of their culture, the Persian men who first recorded Bahá'í history were reluctant to discuss the details of the life of a woman. Such discussion was regarded as highly improper in the Muslim society in which they lived. As a result, the information that we have today about many early Bábí and Bahá'í heroines is scanty.

Only recently have Bahá'ís sought to recover the early history of women in the Faith in any systematic way. The publication of *Khádíjih Bagum: The Wife of the Báb*, by Hand of the Cause Mr. H. M. Balyuzi (George Ronald, 1981) was a beginning. The compilation *Bahíyyih Khánum: The Greatest Holy Leaf*, published at the Bahá'í

World Center (1982), advanced the process. This was followed by a a small volume of the writings of 'Abdu'l-Bahá's wife, *Munírih Khánum: Memoirs and Letters* (Kalimát Press, 1986) and Baharieh Rouhani Ma'ani's *Asíyih Khánum: The Most Exalted Leaf* (George Ronald, 1993). In a similar way, *Black Pearls* (First Edition, 1988) seeks to tell the stories of the early believers who acted as servants in the households of the Báb and Bahá'u'lláh. Here is recorded a small portion of the oral tradition of the Afnán family, the relatives of the Báb. The author, Abu'l Qasim Afnan, a grand-nephew of the Báb, embodies today all of the dignity, the tradition, the spirituality, and the memory of that honored family.

This new willingness to look beyond the traditional story of Bábí history and to explore the history of women and servants in the early days of the Faith has already, at first blush, yielded the most startling discovery: that women and black people were participants in the earliest and most sacred events of Bahá'í history. In *The Dawn-Breakers*, it is recorded that on the evening of May 22, 1844, Mullá Husayn and the Báb were greeted at the door of the Báb's house by his "Ethiopian" servant.* The traditions of the Afnán family inform us that it was the duty of this black servant, Mubárak, to remain awake and attentive to the needs of his Master throughout the night, and that his room was adjacent to that of the Báb. Munírih Khánum, moreover, has related that Khadíjih Bagum, the Báb's wife, likewise remained awake throughout that fateful night, listening to the conversation from the upstairs apartments of the house, where she could hear clearly:

> What an extraordinary night that was! The Báb said to me: "Tonight we will entertain a dear guest." His whole being was ablaze. I was most eager to hear what He had to say, but He turned to me and told me: "It is better if you go and sleep." I did not wish to disobey Him, but I remained awake all night and could hear His blessed voice until the morning, conversing with the Bábu'l-Báb [Mullá Husayn], chanting the verses, and presenting proofs and arguments.**

* "Ethiopian" is a general term here and does not necessarily indicate that this servant was from modern-day Ethiopian lands.

** *Munírih Khánum*, p. 34.

And so we learn that the first night of the Revelation, the Declaration of the Báb, was witnessed and received not only by one man–but also by a woman and an African servant. Although the customs of a Muslim society did not allow these two to sit in the room as the Báb revealed His Mission and initiated a new era of religious history, yet they were present at the event. They heard the Great Announcement. The conventions of nineteenth-century Iranian society dictated that they both had to remain in their separate quarters, apart from Master and guest, as they observed this momentous meeting, but their participation in the event should not be erased.

That the presence of these two silent witnesses to the Declaration of the Báb was overlooked by the first chroniclers of Bahá'í history is understandable. The social positions of women and slaves made them invisible to everyone but the Manifestation of God. They served, quiet and unseen, in the roles allotted to them by the unjust customs of society–customs which were soon to be swept aside in the whirlwind of a New Era. Their only contribution was service.

In the Bahá'í teachings, however, service is recognized as the highest expression of faith. Service to others, and certainly to the Manifestation of God, is the highest condition that a human being can achieve. So important is this concept of servitude that the Center of Bahá'u'lláh's Covenant, His eldest son and chosen successor, took for himself the title of 'Abdu'l-Bahá–meaning servant (or slave) of Bahá'u'lláh. Using this title, 'Abdu'l-Bahá places himself–precisely and literally–in the same condition as the subjects of this book, a servant or slave to the Center of the Faith. This, 'Abdu'l-Bahá insisted, was his real honor, his highest station.

Some Bahá'ís in America felt uncomfortable with this title, as did some Persian believers. These Americans preferred to think of 'Abdu'l-Bahá as the Return of Christ and some continued to refer to him in those terms. In reply he wrote:

> You have written that there is a difference among the believers concerning the 'Second Coming of Christ.' Gracious God! Time and again this question hath arisen . . . My name is 'Abdu'l-Bahá. My qualification is 'Abdu'l-Bahá. My reality is 'Abdu'l-Bahá. My praise

> is ‘Abdu’l-Bahá. Thraldom to the Blessed Perfection is my glorious and refulgent diadem, and servitude to all the human race my perpetual religion . . . No name, no title, no mention, no commendation have I, nor will ever have, except ‘Abdu’l-Bahá. This is my longing. This is my greatest yearning. This is my eternal life. This is my everlasting glory.*

Here ‘Abdu’l-Bahá forcefully rejects any station except the station of service, a station which is available to all people equally.

Both the Báb and Bahá’u’lláh lived in the closed Muslim society of nineteenth-century Iran. Naturally, they spoke the languages of the people and observed many of the customs of the time. For families of means who lived in the cities of Iran, the seclusion of the women of the household was a supreme necessity. Lower class women and female slaves could conduct business in public, but all others were expected–according to strict, orthodox Muslim standards–to remain at home. Many wealthy houses were walled compounds, enclosing trees and pools, and divided

* Quoted in *World Order of Bahá’u’lláh* (Wilmette, Ill.: Bahá’í Publishing Trust, 1938) p. 139.

into two sections–sometimes two separate houses. One section was for men, the *bírúní*; the other for women, the *andarún*. The women of the household were more or less restricted from the male quarters, though they might enter them wearing the veil. Here is where male visitors might be found, the public part of the house. No man who was not a member of the family, or a slave of the household, could enter the women's quarters.

Orthodox Muslims expected that respectable women would seldom venture from the *andarún*. They should leave their houses only occasionally, heavily veiled from head to toe, usually at night to reduce the possibility of being seen; and then only to visit the house of a relative. Any other destination might raise rumors of impropriety, unchastity, or worse. Women of this class were expected to have no contact at all with men, beyond their husbands and immediate relatives, such as fathers, brothers, or sons.

In such a society, domestic slaves were absolutely necessary to carry on the normal business of any household and to maintain the respectability of the family. Strict Muslim codes forbade the women of the family from even answering a knock at the door. Manservants could enter the *andarún*, and so they could attend to the needs of the women of the house. They took care of the daily shopping, conducted the public business of the family, and handled other routine affairs outside the *andarún*. Domestic slaves were usually purchased at a very young age, trained and trusted as members of the family. They generally took their duties seriously and exhibited fierce loyalty to their households. Slaves intended as permanent servants to the family were never sold, of course.

In nineteenth-century Iran, Muslim slaves were often set free, after a period of service, by the families that owned them. Slaves could be freed for extraordinary service, on special occasions, or as an act of generosity upon the death of their masters. 'Abdu'l-Bahá recalled that this practice had been followed in Bahá'u'lláh's household. The family's slaves had been manumitted after the passing of Bahá'u'lláh's father, for example. 'Abdu'l-Bahá relates the story like this:

FOREWORD

> My grandfather had many colored maids and servants. When the Blessed Perfection [Bahá'u'lláh] became the head of the family, he liberated all of them, and gave them permission to leave or stay, but if they desired to remain it would, of course, be in a different manner. However, all of them, revelling in their new-found freedom preferred to leave, except Isfandíyár, who remained in the household and continued to serve us with proverbial faithfulness and chastity.*

This book is a first attempt to recover the histories of the servants in the households of the Báb and Bahá'u'lláh. The story of Isfandíyár is among them.

ANTHONY A. LEE
LOS ANGELES

* From *Star of the West*, vol. IX (March 21, 1918) no. 1, p. 38.

PREFACE

by Abu'l-Qasim Afnan

UNTIL QUITE RECENTLY in human history, slavery has been prevalent throughout the world. Everywhere, in times of war and aggression, innocent people were captured, takPen into bondage, and sold as slaves. These customs were so deep-rooted that the major religions sanctioned and even institutionalized the practice of slavery. In the Jewish scriptures, slavery was made lawful, but subjected to regulations. (See Lev. 25: 39-55) And the Apostle Paul, in the New Testament, appears to have condoned it. (1 Tim. 6:23) Later, in the fifteenth century, Nicholas V gave papal sanction for the Portuguese, under Henry the

Navigator, to capture and enslave pagans. There seems little doubt that the prophet Muhammad never looked favorably on the practice of slavery; at most he only tolerated it. Nonetheless, there are numerous passages in the Qur'an which Muslims have taken to endorse the ownership of slaves. (Sura 4 [Women]:91; Sura 24 [Light]:30-32; Sura 90 [The City]:12; Sura 33 [The Confederates]:49-51) But, it was a freed slave, Bilál ibn Ribáh, the Ethiopian, whom Muhammad designated as the first muezzin of Islam even though he was a stutterer, and when chanting the *adhán*, the call to prayer, he would pronounce the letter "sh" as "s."

It was only toward the end of the eighteenth century that so-called civilized man first thought seriously of abolishing the institution of human slavery. The first attempt of the French legislature in 1794, to enforce a law outlawing slavery ended in failure. The British, through much of the nineteenth century, waged a battle against the practice in the Middle East and elsewhere. Most of their efforts proved futile, however, until the Pen of Bahá'u'lláh issued the divine decree and proclaimed unequivocally the law of God.

During the 1800s, throughout the Middle East, but particularly in Iran and in the Ottoman Empire, slavery flourished. The victims were not restricted to any special class, race, or color. Dark-skinned Africans and white-skinned Georgians or Caucasians might be included among the common slaves in the cities of Iran, even though the white slaves usually received preferential treatment and lived under better conditions.

These slaves were normally captives brought to Iran from foreign lands. Most of these unfortunates went through life remembering and cherishing their homelands and their mother tongues. There arose, in consequence, a small but beautiful mixture of languages in Persia which even found expression in poetry. One Bahá'í poet, Shúrídih Shírází, who has eulogized both 'Abdu'l-Bahá and Mírzá Abú'l-Fadl, wrote a charming poem in this mixed creole language.

Slaves were a part of every wealthy household. Dirty and menial tasks were their daily work, and they could be treated cruelly. The rulers made eunuchs of young boys and took them into the women's quarters of their palaces as servants. The eunuchs were respected and trusted by the ladies of the household and were often taken into their full confidence. Unlike ordinary slaves, these eunuchs sometimes came to occupy places of prominence in society.

Not until the revelation of the Kitáb-i Aqdas by Bahá'u'lláh (1873) was the practice of slavery condemned and forbidden to all believers. But before this, in His Tablet to Queen Victoria, Bahá'u'lláh had promised the queen a great reward because of the efforts of her government to abolish trading in slaves.

Here are collected the stories of those black slaves who found the Most Great Revelation and came to serve the families of the Báb and Bahá'u'lláh at various times. Despite their unfortunate condition, they each attained to the highest station of spirit in this life, receiving the assurance of the pleasure and acceptance of the Holy Ones.

I wish to express my deepest gratitude to Farzad Katirai who kindly translated this article from Persian into English. I am also grateful to Khazeh Fananapazir who assisted with the translation. I must also thank Foad Ashraf who translated into English the reminiscences of Badí'í Bushrú'í regarding Isfandíyár, the servant of Bahá'u'lláh.

ABU'L-QASIM AFNAN
OXFORD, ENGLAND

BLACK PEARLS

Servants in the Households of the Báb and Bahá'u'lláh

SECOND EDITION

THE HOUSE OF THE BÁB IN SHIRAZ,
the upper chamber

Bahá'í World Centre

HÁJÍ MUBÁRAK

RECORDS INDICATE that both sides of the family of the Báb (paternal and maternal), in keeping with their social position and the customs of the time, owned black slaves. The behavior of both families toward their slaves, however, was reputed to have been exceptional. They were unfailing in their generosity and kindness, and it was often said of them that they treated their servants just as members of their own families.*

In 1842, upon His return to His home in Shiraz from a six-year sojourn in Bushihr and Karbala,

* The last slave purchased by my forefathers was a Swahili youth named Salmán. He was acquired in Shiraz around 1870, well before the revelation of the Kitáb-i Aqdas in which Bahá'u'lláh forbids slavery. Eventually, Salmán was sent to serve in the family of Dá'í Husayn, a remarkable Bahá'í who lived in the town of Ábádih. Salmán's descendants can still be traced.

Bahá'í World Centre

THE HOUSE OF THE BÁB IN SHIRAZ,
the room of Mubárak.

the Báb–as was the custom–acquired a young Ethiopian slave. The man was nineteen years old and was named Mubárak (meaning, blessed). The bill of purchase, which still exists among the Báb's business accounts, is dated 1842 and indicates that the price paid was fourteen *túmáns* (about twenty-eight dollars).

Hájí Mírzá Abú'l-Qásím, the brother-in-law of the Báb,* had purchased Mubárak from slave traders when he was a child of only five years and had adopted him into his own family. The education and upbringing that Mubárak received was exemplary. The Báb, approving of his instruction and his abilities, purchased him and brought him to the holy household. His quarters were arranged in the southern courtyard of the Báb's house.

I VIVIDLY REMEMBER that my grandmother, the daughter of Hájí Mírzá Abú'l-Qásím, would often recall Mubárak's extreme modesty and politeness. She would say that, while intelligent, quick of

* The great-grandfather of Shoghi Effendi, the Guardian of the Bahá'í Faith.

understanding, and possessing a great capacity to learn, he nonetheless displayed the utmost meekness and humility and showed kindness to all. She would describe his manners and demeanor as being regal, and would remark that they well befitted his service in the holy house. More than anything else, though, she remembered him as a loyal and faithful servant of the Báb and His mother.

BY THE TIME OF HIS RETURN to Shiraz in 1842, the Báb had largely discontinued His commercial activities. Those business affairs that remained were attended to at the offices of His uncle. Here, Mubárak was of assistance. He was entrusted with the task of settling the Báb's outstanding accounts, and he discharged his duties with superb competence. More importantly, it was Mubárak who had the signal distinction, on the afternoon of May 22, 1844, of receiving and welcoming into the home of the Báb, with his unique warmth and affection, his Master and Mullá Husayn, who that night would become the first believer in the new Revelation. Nabíl-i A'zam, the Bahá'í historian, recounts in *The Dawn-Breakers* how the Báb, met Mullá Husayn that day outside the city of Shiraz and invited him to His home. Mullá Husayn continues:

> "'We soon found ourselves standing at the gate of a house of modest appearance. He [the Báb] knocked at the door, which was soon opened by an Ethiopian servant. "Enter therein in peace, secure,"* were His words as He crossed the threshold and motioned me to follow Him. His invitation, uttered with power and majesty, penetrated my soul. I thought it a good augury to be addressed in such words, standing as I did on the threshold of the first house I was entering in Shiráz, a city the very atmosphere of which had produced already an indescribable impression upon me. Might not my visit to this house, I thought to myself, enable me to draw nearer to the Object of my quest?'"**

It was none other than Mubárak who, throughout that night, the night of the revelation of the Báb's station waited, sleepless and vigilant, just outside the chamber, ready to serve when called upon.

* Qur'an 15:46.

** Quoted in [Nabíl-i A'zam], *The Dawn Breakers* (Wilmette, Ill.: Bahá'í Publishing Trust, 1932) trans. by Shoghi Effendi, pp. 53-54.

Bahá'í World Centre

ENTRANCE TO THE HOUSE OF THE BÁB
in Shiraz. This door was opened by Mubárak to
welcome Mullá Husayn and the other
Letters of the Living.

In *The Dawn-Breakers*, Nabíl records Mullá Husayn as having said:

> "'During those days I was, on several occasions, summoned by the Báb to visit Him. He would send at night-time that same Ethiopian servant to the masjid [the mosque where Mullá Husayn resided], bearing to me His most loving message of welcome. Every time I visited Him, I spent the entire night in His presence. Wakeful until dawn, I sat at His feet fascinated by the charm of His utterance and oblivious to the world and its cares and pursuits.'"*

It was also Mubárak who was found by Mullá Husayn, at the hour of dawn, standing outside the gates of the holy house, waiting to greet the arrival of the second Letter of the Living, Mullá 'Alíy-i Bastámí. Mullá Husayn had been charged by the Báb to reveal His station to no one. Eighteen disciples, the Báb had promised, each independently, unwarned and uninvited, would find Him. Nabíl tells the story of the second disciple:

> . . . whilst wrapt in prayer, Mullá 'Alíy-i Bastámí had a vision. There appeared before his eyes a light, and, lo! that light moved off before him. Allured by its splen-

* Quoted in *The Dawn-Breakers*, p. 66.

> dour, he followed it, till at last it led him to his promised Beloved. At that very hour, in the mid-watches of the night, he arose and, exultant with joy and radiant with gladness, opened the door of his chamber and hastened to Mullá Husayn. He threw himself into the arms of his revered companion. Mullá Husayn most lovingly embraced him and said: "Praise be to God who hath guided us hither! We had not been guided had not God guided us!"
>
> That very morning, at break of day, Mullá Husayn, followed by Mullá 'Alí, hastened to the residence of the Báb. At the entrance of His house they met the faithful Ethiopian servant, who immediately recognised them and greeted them in these words: "Ere break of day, I was summoned to the presence of my Master, who instructed me to open the door of the house and to stand expectant at its threshold. 'Two guests,' He said, 'are to arrive early this morning. Extend to them in My name a warm welcome. Say to them from Me: "Enter therein in the name of God." ' "*

Throughout the eventful months which followed, Mubárak dedicated himself to serving the Letters of the Living and the other believers who journeyed to Shiraz. He served them both in the holy house and in the home of Hájí Mírzá Sayyid 'Alí, later known as Khál-i A'zam, the uncle of the

* Quoted in *The Dawn-Breakers*, p. 68.

Báb who eventually would die a martyr's death.*
So trusted was Mubárak that the Báb, during this time, committed numerous Tablets and verbal instructions–some addressed to the Letters of the Living–to his care for safe delivery.

When the number of the Letters of the Living was complete–when all eighteen of the first disciples had found Him–the Báb summoned each of them and assigned to each a mission intended to proclaim the new Faith. As for the Báb Himself, He prepared to embark on a pilgrimage to Mecca. The only believers who were given the privilege of accompanying Him were Quddús, the first in rank among the Letters of the Living, and Mubárak.

THROUGHOUT THE WHOLE of that strenuous journey, Mubárak never parted from his Master. He continually received the Báb's blessings and expressions of appreciation. On one occasion, en

* Hájí Mírzá Sayyid 'Alí was executed in Tehran in 1850, and is counted as one of the Seven Martyrs of Tehran. See *The Dawn-Breakers*, p. 446-49.

route to the pilgrimage, as related by Nabíl,* a saddlebag containing many of the Báb's Tablets and holy Writings was stolen. This account of the incident was narrated by Mubárak himself:

> "At dawn, His Holiness broke His journey near a well. I unpacked the loads from the backs of the camels and prepared to settle down. Just as the Báb began to pray, a bedouin appeared as swift as lightning, snatched the saddlebag filled with the papers of the Báb, and fled. I immediately gave chase, hoping to apprehend him and retrieve the documents. In the midst of His prayers, however, the Báb motioned me to desist, and after His prayers were completed, He showered much affection and kindness upon me, assuring me that God would grant my recompense, as all goodly deeds are rewarded by Him. He continued to speak, saying that, had I pursued him, the Arab could not have escaped. But Divine Providence intended that these papers would, by means of his actions, come to reach such persons as would not otherwise be possible. Then addressing me, He said: 'Grieve not at his action, for this was decreed by God, the Ordainer, the Almighty.' "

As part of the ritual of Muslim pilgrimage, while in Mecca, the Báb sacrificed nineteen lambs–nine in His own name, seven in the name

* Quoted in *The Dawn-Breakers*, p. 132.

of Quddús, and three for Mubárak, securing for him too the full rites of pilgrimage.

The Báb remained in Mecca for twenty-seven days and then spent the same length of time in Medina. Afterwards, He and His companions embarked for Muscat by way of Jidda. The Báb had earlier, on his journey to Mecca, become acquainted with the Sultan of Muscat and had received an invitation to stay at his home on the return journey. There are documents to indicate that the Báb remained in Muscat for a month and a half, for all of the month of Rabí'u'th-Thání and the first half of the month of Jamádíyu'l-Avval. During His sojourn, voluminous writings emanated from His pen and the newborn Faith was proclaimed to the chief clergymen of Najaf, Karbala, Bushihr, and Muscat. The recipient of one of His epistles was the erudite Shaykh Sulaymán, the mujtahid of Muscat.

On Friday, the seventh of Jamádíyu'th-Thání (June 4, 1845), the Báb arrived in Bushihr on the last leg of His journey home. He remained only a few days, and on the afternoon of Wednesday, the nineteenth of the same month, He departed for

Shiraz, accompanied by Mubárak. A cousin of the Báb, Hájí Mírzá Muhammad Taqí, Vakílu'd-Dawlih,* has recorded in a letter the story of that departure:

> Despite repeated imploring by my father [Hájí Mírzá Sayyid Muḥammad**] that the Báb extend His stay in Bushihr, his request was not granted, and the Báb departed on the appointed day. His uncle was despondent on account of the Báb's leaving and wished that his nephew had remained. But later it became known that horsemen had been sent from Shiraz to arrest the Báb. He had refused to delay his departure, and therefore He encountered the soldiers enroute. Otherwise His beloved uncle would have had to witness the sad events destined to befall Him.
>
> Once He had left Bushihr, the haste with which He departed was soon diminished. The distance between Bushihr and Kunár-Takhtih, which is no more than fifty kilometers, took five days to cover. It was while the Báb was in the latter village that the horsemen dispatched from Shiraz by Husayn Khán, the governor, arrived.

Throughout the remaining distance to Shiraz, the soldiers escorting the Báb were served and

* He later became the chief builder of the Mashriqu'l-Adhkár in Ashkhabad, Russian Turkmenistan.

** The uncle of the Báb to whom the Kitáb-í Íqán was later addressed by Bahá'u'lláh.

cared for by Mubárak with the thoroughness and courtesy that distinguished his every action. Later on in that same journey, Mubárak broke away from the company of his Master to arrive in Shiraz some two hours earlier than the Báb and His guards. He was able to alert the Báb's uncle, Hájí Mírzá Sayyid 'Alí, to the imminent arrival of the Báb and the circumstances surrounding it. As a result, the uncle was able to be present when his nephew was conducted into the presence of Husayn Khán, the governor of Fars.

The next twenty-eight months of the Báb's residence in Shiraz were difficult times for all in the Báb's household. Mubárak shared fully in the anxieties and tensions of those trying months. His Master was placed under house arrest, and Hájí Mírzá Sayyid 'Alí was pledged to insure His seclusion. Therefore, the Báb took up residence in the house of His uncle. An interior door leading to the house of the mother-in-law of the Báb, however, was kept secret. Through this door, the Báb was accessible. During this period, Mubárak would guide the believers who were to be granted an audience through the adjacent house into His presence.

When the Báb left Shiraz for Isfahan, He committed the care of His mother and His wife to Mubárak and to Fiddih (pronounced fez-ZEH), the maidservant of the household. He expressed the wish that they would endeavor to the best of their abilities to comfort them in His absence. So, despite his own intense attachment to the Báb and the suffering he had to endure in his separation from his Lord, Mubárak found himself in the position of having to console and cheer the mother, the grandmother, and the wife of the Báb.

THE BÁB WAS MARTYRED in Tabriz on July 9, 1850, but the news of these dire events was kept from the women and the servants of the holy household. Naturally, as was the custom in wealthy families, the women lived secluded in their houses, except for visits to the homes of friends and relatives. It was more than a year after the martyrdom when circumstances came to the point that the secret could be kept no longer. Now, the women of the family learned of both the martyrdom of the Báb and that of his uncle, Hájí

Mírzá Sayyid 'Alí, in Tehran, at the same time.* The mother of the Báb was beside herself with grief.

To these calamities were added the spiteful words and malicious attitude of certain ill-wishers and mischief-makers within the family in Shiraz who had always been hostile to the Báb. Unable to bear these injuries any longer, the mother and the grandmother of the Báb decided to transfer their residence to Karbala. They selected a number of loyal and devoted believers to accompany them. Faithful Mubárak was asked by the mother of the Báb to join the entourage on the journey to Iraq.

Even until the time of his death, Mubárak was not told of the Báb's martyrdom. Likewise, the other servants of the household remained in ignorance of these events. The family wanted neither to distress them nor to allow their servants, who were the only ones of the house who were regularly seen in the marketplace, to become the

* See H. M. Balyuzi, *Khadíjih Bagum: The Wife of the Báb* (Oxford: George Ronald, 1981) pp. 25-28.

source of delusive news or rumors. Both Mubárak and Fiddih were told that the Báb had voyaged to India to manage his mercantile affairs and would eventually return.

While in Karbala, Mubárak longed for the return of his Master. He made a broom to which he attached a green handle. Green is the color of Muhammad's lineage: since the Báb was a descendant of the Prophet, Mubárak's broom was made in remembrance of Him. Every morning at the hour of dawn, Mubárak would use the broom to sweep the courtyard around the sanctuary of the Shrine of Imám Husayn. He vowed to perform this pious deed every day until the Báb would return. After completing this exercise, he would then proceed to procure the provisions required by the household and complete his other duties.

Mubárak was about forty years old when he came to Karbala with the mother of the Báb. Not long after this, however, he passed away, leaving his mistress deeply grieved. He was buried on the grounds of the Shrine of the Imám Husayn. It is his everlasting honor that his Lord was pleased with his deeds and services.

Baha'i World Center

THE HOUSE OF THE BÁB IN SHIRAZ,

doorway and stairs leading to the upper chamber.

FIDDIH

FIDDIH (pronounced fez-ZEH) was an Ethiopian girl of tender years probably no older than seven when she was acquired by the Báb to be trained to serve in His household and to attend His wife. She was educated by the mother and the wife of the Báb, receiving instruction from both. At an early age, she showed a prodigious mastery of manners and etiquette. She excelled in the culinary arts and acquired a reputation for excellent needlework and embroidery. She was also faithful to her religious duties.

From the start, Fiddih was regarded by all of the Báb's relatives as a member of their family and was treated accordingly. She herself was enthralled by the wife of the Báb, Khadíjih Bagum, who also loved her dearly. Such was their affection for one another that neither could bear to be separated from the other for even a short while.

As Fiddih grew up, she began to assist in the household. The wife of the Báb confided in her fully, and all of Khadíjih Bagum's precious belongings were left in Fiddih's care. While the mother of the Báb lived in Shiraz, Fiddih also devoted much of her time to nursing her and looking after every detail of her life. After her departure for Karbala, Fiddih was able to dedicate herself fully to Khadíjih Bagum to the exception of all others in her life. She never developed any warm friendship with anyone else, even though there were many other servants in the homes of the uncles of the Báb. Never would she appear in public except in attendance on Khadíjih Bagum.

During the fifteen days when the future wife of 'Abdu'l-Bahá, Munírih Khánum, and her companions were the guests of Khadíjih Bagum in the house of the uncle of the Báb, Fiddih attended them as well.* In a letter addressed to Khadíjih

* See Munírih Khánum, *Munírih Khánum: Memoirs and Letters* (Los Angeles: Kalimát Press, 1986) pp. 26-37.

Bagum from the Holy Land, Munírih Khánum mentions Fiddih many times. She sends her warm greetings and expresses gratitude for her services.

Like Mubárak, Fiddih was never told of the martyrdom of the Báb. In 1877, at the command of Bahá'u'lláh, repairs were begun on the house of the Báb in Shiraz so that Khadíjih Bagum could live there once again. Fiddih was found rejoicing: she imagined that the repairs were being undertaken in anticipation of the Báb's return from His extended journey. Her joy was a heartbreaking testimony to her devotion. She had a pure soul and her spirit was abrim with love. Although she was not aware of the station and mission of the Báb, she was so enchanted by Him that she could not even fathom the thought that He could have been killed under such brutal circumstances.

FIDDIH REFUSED to even contemplate life without Khadíjih Bagum. She would always ask her mistress to pray that she would not continue to live after her beloved lady. In her own prayers, she could be heard to supplicate God to accept her

Bahá'í World Center

ROOM IN THE HOUSE OF THE BAB,
once occupied by the wife of the Báb, Khadijih Bagum

wish that, so long as He destined for the wife of the Báb to remain in this mortal world, Fiddih too might remain to serve her; but she begged never to see the day when her lady was no longer with her.

An account of the closing hours of Fiddih's life is contained in a letter written by Hájí Mírzá 'Abdu'lláh Khán* addressed to his wife and conveying the news of the passing of the wife of the Báb. At three and a half hours after sunset on Sunday, November 15, 1881, Khadíjih Bagum left this earthly realm. While arrangements were still in progress for her funeral and interment, true to her soul's desire, the spirit of Fiddih winged its flight to join her beloved mistress. She was about forty-seven at the time of her death.** Her mortal remains were laid in the precincts of the tomb of Bíbí Dukhtarán, a matron saint, near the grave of the Báb's infant son, Ahmad.

AFTER FORTY YEARS of loyal and devoted service to the wife of the Báb, Fiddih's prayer was

* A paternal uncle of Muvaqqarid-Dawlih, the father of the Hand of the Cause Mr. Hasan M. Balyuzi.

** Both Khadíjih Bagum and Fiddih died of dysentery.

accepted and her wish granted. She passed away on the night of Khadíjih Bagum's ascension to the Abhá Kingdom. In a Tablet, Bahá'u'lláh greatly favors her, assuring her of divine forgiveness.

The Tablet was revealed in honor of Khadíjih Bagum. I will paraphrase a short passage from that Tablet:

> O thou who are the fruit of the Tree of My Life! Thy tribulations have caused the ocean of sorrow to surge and the breezes of forgiveness to waft. I testify that, as a blessing and bounty on Our part to thee, God hath forgiven every servant and maidservant who ascended on the eve or the day of thine ascension to the Abhá Horizon, the Exalted Paradise, save for those who have denied His rights and rejected what hath been manifested from Him to all men.
>
> Thus hath God chosen thee, O My Leaf, for this most great bounty and this foremost and primal rank.

ISFANDÍYÁR

AMONG THE SERVANTS in the household of Bahá'-u'lláh in Tehran was a black man, Isfandíyár. When the terrible persecutions of Bábís began, and Bahá'u'lláh was arrested and cast into a dungeon, Isfandíyár proved to be His only true and loyal manservant. He remained in the household to serve the holy family, despite great danger to his own life. Bahíyyih Khánum, the Greatest Holy Leaf, the daughter of Bahá'u'lláh, has related the story of her father's arrest:

> One day I remember very well, though I was only six years old at the time. It seemed that an attempt had been made on the life of the Sháh by a half-crazy young Bábí.
>
> My father was away at his country house in the village of [Níyávarán], which was his property, the vil-

lagers of which were all and individually cared for by him.

Suddenly and hurriedly a servant came rushing in great distress to my mother.

"The master, the master, he is arrested. I have seen him! He has walked many miles! Oh, they have beaten him! They say he has suffered the torture of the bastinado! His feet are bleeding! He has no shoes on! His turban has gone! His clothes are torn! There are chains upon his neck!"

My poor mother's face grew whiter and whiter.

We children were terribly frightened and could only weep bitterly.

Immediately everybody, all our relations and friends, and servants fled from our house in terror, only one manservant, Isfandíyár, remained, and one woman. Our palace, and the smaller houses belonging to it, were very soon stripped of everything; furniture, treasures, all were stolen by the people.*

More about this noble servant can be found in the memoirs of Badí'í Bushrú'í, who lived in the presence of 'Abdu'l-Bahá for many years. He relates the story as he heard it from 'Abdu'l-Bahá:

The period of tribulation in Tehran [after the attempt on the life of the shah in 1852] has already been men-

* Quoted in Lady Blomfield, *The Chosen Highway* (Wilmette, Ill.: Bahá'í Publishing Trust, 1967) pp. 40-41.

tioned. One thousand persons were killed, and the Blessed Beauty [Bahá'u'lláh] was cast into prison. He had a black servant named Isfandíyár who was the embodiment of all good qualities; and He had another black servant called Mubárak* who was completely the opposite. Isfandíyár had been entrusted with all of the confidential affairs of the Blessed Beauty.

It was suggested to the shah that if Isfandíyár were arrested, he could be made to reveal all this secret information. Therefore, a plan was hatched to find Isfandíyár. Sulaymán Khán [a prominent Bábí of Tehran who was arrested and martyred during the persecutions of this period] had a servant named 'Abbás who knew all the Bábís. Accompanied by fifty or sixty soldiers, 'Abbás was taken around the city, and he pointed out about thirty believers.

'Abdu'l-Bahá's mother** sent Isfandíyár away to Mazandaran [in northern Iran] where he might be safe. But he returned a week later. When asked why he had come back, he said: "I have debts to pay to the butcher and the baker in town. I don't want people to say, 'That servant of the Blessed Beauty has swindled us and run away.' I will not leave until all my debts are paid." And so he went through the city, sparing no effort to pay off all his obligations.

One day, while he was walking in the bazaar, 'Abbás with his government escort came upon Isfandíyár. 'Abbás saluted him with great formality, but he did not denounce him to the soldiers.

* He should not be confused with Hájí Mubárak, the servant of the Báb, whose story is told in the first chapter of this book.
** Asíyih Khánum, the wife of Bahá'u'lláh.

Eventually, Isfandíyár returned to Mazandaran. Upon his arrival, the governor of the province, Mírzá Yahyá Khán, who knew him, engaged him as his head servant and placed all the affairs of his household in his hands. Some time later, when Mírzá Yahyá Khán and his entourage stopped in Baghdad on their way to pilgrimage to the holy cities, Isfandíyár had the privilege of visiting Bahá'u'lláh there. He begged for permission to remain in His presence.

The Blessed Beauty said to him: "Behold! This noble person gave you a refuge in his house when you were a fugitive. I do not now wish you to prove unfaithful to him and leave unless he approves."

Isfandíyár sent someone to Yahyá Khán on his behalf to beg to be released from service. But his master replied that he would never consent to let him go. And so, Isfandíyár stayed with Yahyá Khán. They returned to Mazandaran.

Isfandíyár, that unique and peerless servant, passed away in Mazandaran.*

'Abdu'l-Bahá has explained that the debts Isfandíyár paid after Bahá'u'lláh's arrest were not really his own, but were actually the debts of the holy household that he had incurred in the marketplace during the normal course of his duties.

* Cf. 'Abdu'l-Bahá, *The Promulgation of Universal Peace,* Second Edition (Wilmette, Ill.: Bahá'í Publishing Trust, 1982) pp. 426-27.

Nonetheless, he remained in Tehran for one full month, at a time when anyone even suspected of being a Bábí could be arrested and killed. He walked openly in the streets and bazaars; he sold his own possessions; and he found that he could earn a little money. Gradually, he paid all the creditors of the Blessed Beauty in full. Not a single penny remained unpaid. Then he presented himself to the holy family and bade them farewell; and only then did he quit the city.*

Many years later, while touring America, 'Abdu'l-Bahá gave this testimony to the services of this loyal servant:

> If a perfect man could be found in the world, that man was Isfandíyár. He was the essence of love, radiant with sanctity and perfection, luminous with light. Whenever I think of Isfandíyár, I am moved to tears, although he passed away fifty years ago.**

* Ibid.

** Ibid., p. 426. Nabíl has related this story of his experience in the house of Bahá'u'lláh (c. 1849) sometime before the martyrdom of the Báb: "On another occasion, when I visited that same house, I was on the point of entering the room that Mírzá Yahyá occupied, when Áqáy-i-Kalím, whom I had previously met, approached and requested me, since Isfandíyár, their servant, had gone to market and had not yet returned, to conduct 'Áqá ['Abdu'l-Bahá, who was at this time a child of six] to the Madrisiy-i-Mírzá-Sálih in his stead and then return to this place. I gladly consented, and as I was preparing to leave, I saw the Most Great Branch, a child of exquisite beauty, wearing the kuláh [a lambskin hat] and cloaked in the jubbiy-i-hizári'í [a kind of overcoat], emerge from the room which His Father occupied, and descend the steps leading to the gate of the house. I advanced and stretched forth my arms to carry Him. 'We shall walk together,' He said, as He took hold of my hand and led me out of the house. We chatted together as we walked hand in hand in the direction of the madrisih known in those days by the name of Pá-Minár. As we reached His classroom, He turned to me and said: Come again this afternoon and take me back to my home, for Isfandíyár is unable to fetch me. My Father will need him to-day.' I gladly acquiesced, and returned immediately to the house of Bahá'u'lláh." (*The Dawn-Breakers,* p. 441.)

ش جناب مسعود

بنام خداوند یکتا

یا مسعود مظلوم عالم از مقام محمود به تو توجّه نموده و ترا ذکر مینماید
چه که زفرات ترا در فراق مشاهده نمودیم و عبرات ترا در هجر نیّر آفاق
دیدیم انّ ربّک هو الحقّ علّام الغیوب به خاطر آر آن حینی را که مظلوم به محلّ تو
آمد اردت لقائه حضر امام وجهک از حقّ می طلبیم ترا بر حفظ این مقام
مؤیّد فرماید انّ الملوک و المملوک فی الحقّ سوآء مراتب نفوس
هر یک به مقدار بوده و هست انّ اکرمکم عند الله اتقاکم شاهد و گواه
انّا نوصیک بحبّ افنانی الّذین وفوا بعهدی و میثاقی و قاموا علی خدمة
امری النّبأ العظیم البهآء علی اهل البهآء الّذین ما غرّتهم الدّنیا و ما منعتهم شبهات
العلمآء و ما اضعفتهم شوکة الامرآء اقبلوا بقلوب نورآء الی الله ربّ الارباب.

PERSIAN TABLET OF BAHÁ'U'LLÁH
revealed in honor of Mas'úd. See p. 38.

Calligraphy by M. Moughen

MAS'ÚD

AMONG THE BLACK SERVANTS trained under the benefaction of the uncle of the Báb, Khál-i Akbar, was Mas'úd who recognized the station of Bahá'-u'lláh, became a steadfast believer, and even attained to the holy presence. The Báb's uncle had purchased Mas'úd when he was but a youth from slave traders who abducted him from Zanzibar. He gave him the name *mas'úd,* which means fortunate or felicitous. Khál-i Akbar paid for his schooling in a *maktab,* a traditional grammar school. Here, Mas'úd acquired a basic education, with a good grasp of arithmetic and diction. He spoke with the accent of his native land, though, and always found it difficult to enunciate certain numbers. Over the years, he became renowned in Shiraz as a sportsman, and particularly for excellent horsemanship. Mas'úd enjoyed cooking and would often prepare exquisite dishes which were admired by all.

In manners, demeanor, in all respects of propriety, and in relations with others, Mas'úd was meticulous. For this, Khál-i Akbar favored him with special affection and endeavored to teach him the Faith. Mas'úd was sincerely attracted and soon ranked among the foremost believers in Shiraz.

He was always a dependable assistant to the Báb's uncle, who trusted him and would confide in him totally. He, moreover, was a faithful assistant to the wife of the Báb. After the departure of Mubárak, it was Mas'úd who attended to all matters that required attention outside the house. His loyalty and devotion to the family were also unaffected by the death of Khál-i Akbar.

WHEN THE YOUNGER DAUGHTER of the Báb's uncle was granted permission to visit Bahá'u'lláh in the Holy Land, Mas'úd was chosen to accompany her and serve as her guide and protector. They were instructed to first embark on a pilgrimage to Mecca, and thenceforth to proceed to the Holy Land. Mas‘úd remained in ‘Akká for six months. He was captivated by Bahá’u’lláh. When in the presence of the Blessed Beauty, he would become lost in wonderment as he surrendered himself to His life-giving words.

On one occasion, while in the Holy Land, he invited Bahá’u’lláh to a feast which he hosted, and he sought permission to prepare those dishes he was wont to prepare in Shiraz. Bahá’u’lláh consented and thereby conferred a unique honor upon Mas‘úd.

It was Mas‘úd’s wish to remain in ‘Akká to serve in the household of Bahá’u’lláh. His request was eventually presented to the Blessed Beauty, but He advised that Mas‘úd should return to Shiraz and continue to serve in the household of Khál-i Akbar. He obeyed, and he escorted his charge–Khál’s daughter–back home by way of Beirut. In Lebanon, they spent several months with the Afnán-i Kabír (the Great Afnán)* and

* Hájí Mírzá Sayyid Hasan, the brother of the wife of the Báb. His wife had a major role in the early training and instruction of Mas‘úd.

his wife, who was also a daughter of Khál-i Akbar. From there, they returned to Shiraz by way of Bombay.

After his return to Shiraz, Mas'úd became greatly distressed by his separation from Bahá'u'lláh. His depression became so intense that it could not be controlled. He withdrew from the society of his friends and secluded himself. Unable to contain his pangs of sorrow, he finally sent a supplication to his Lord, pouring out his innermost feeling of grief and despair. In reply, he was honored with a Tablet from the pen of Bahá'u'lláh which I will paraphrase:

> Shíráz, To his honor Mas'úd.
> In the Name of God, the Single, the Incomparable!
>
> O Mas'úd! The Wronged One of the World [Bahá'u'lláh] hath turned His countenance to thee from this Station, the All-Glorious, the All-Praised. We make mention of thee, inasmuch as We have witnessed thy lamentations on account of they remoteness from Him Who is the Central Orb of the universe. Verily, thy Lord is the True One, the Knower of things unseen.
>
> Recall thou the time when this Wronged One came to thy home. Thou wished to meet with Him, and He came to thee–into thy home. We beseech the one true God to aid thee to preserve this distinction.

Verily, before the one true God, they who are the rulers and lords of men and they that are their subjects and vassals are equal and the same. The ranks of all men are dependent on their potential and capacity. Witness unto this truth are the words, "In Truth, they are most honored before God who are most righteous."

We exhort thee to show love toward the Afnán who have fulfilled my Covenant and Testament and who have arisen to serve my Cause, the Mighty, Most Great.

All glory be upon the people of Bahá whom the changes and chances of this world have not misled, whom the doubts and misgivings of the divines have not hindered, and who have not been weakened by the might and power of earthly rulers. These are the people of Bahá who have turned toward God, the Lord of Lords, with hearts that are radiant and luminous.

THE FAMILY OF Khál-i Akbar made every effort to comfort and console Mas'úd in his depression. They insisted that he must marry, hoping that his new life would make him less despondent and sad. Although he felt spiritually unprepared for marriage, he acceded to their wishes and married an Ethiopian girl named Gulchihrih (gol-cheh-REH), who was also a servant in Khál's household. To them was born a daughter whom they named Sa'ídih (sa-eed-EH).

Despite his new family and the love and devotion that he showed to his wife and daughter, Mas‘úd longed only for another opportunity to attain the presence of Bahá’u’lláh. Soon after his marriage, he ascended to the Abhá Kingdom.

I REMEMBER GULCHIHRIH distinctly. She was a tall, slender woman with an attractive face. She was jolly, talkative and very fond of the water pipe. She came to the house of my father to care for my mother, and she lived with us for many years until her death.

Gulchihrih remembered her home and her childhood days in Africa. She would hold me on her lap and tell me about her life before she was taken as a slave. Not once was she able to finish her story without my breaking down and weeping for her. She would lovingly describe the wide, tree-lined avenues of her native town and the large home in which she lived.

She would say: “There was a brook running near our house where I would play with my brothers and sisters. Our parents warned us to beware of white men. One day, while playing with my friends, we spotted two camel riders approaching. As they drew near, the older children recognized who they were and fled. I could not keep up with them and was soon caught. One of them put a knife to my throat and threatened me. I dared not say a word. They took me away, and eventually I was shipped to Bushihr." She would describe her father and mother, and aunts and uncles, and the love that existed among them. She remembered also that she had a newborn brother who was very dear to her.

Unfortunately, she knew nothing of the Faith that had been the center of her husband's life. Sa'ídih, however, became a believer and was well versed in the teachings. She married Faraj, also in the household of Khál. Their union coincided with the marriage of my two uncles, and it was decided that all three celebrations would be held together. A grand wedding feast was held in honor of all three couples. Her marriage produced only one son, who was named Mas'úd in honor of his grandfather. This Mas'úd lived happily in Shiraz until 1968.

Baha'i World Centre

'ABDU'L-BAHÁ'S RESIDENCE IN 'AKKÁ

known as the House of 'Abdu'lláh Páshá. Shown here in 1912

SÁLIH ÁQÁ

I OFTEN HEARD MY FATHER* tell the story of Sálih Áqá the Berber, a servant in the house of 'Abdu'l-Bahá whose sincerity and devotion became legendary. After the ascension of Bahá'u'lláh,** Bahíyyih Khánum, the Greatest Holy Leaf–'Abdu'l-Bahá's sister–was deeply grieved and depressed. Seeing her in this condition, 'Abdu'l-Bahá recommended that she leave the Holy Land for a short while. Accordingly, she journeyed to Cairo in 1894, and spent several months there.

Hájí Mírzá Hasan Khurásání, a prominent Bahá'í, at the request of the Master, acted as the host of the Greatest Holy Leaf during her sojourn

* Hájí Mírzá Habibu'lláh Afnán, the late custodian of the holy House of the Báb.
** May 29, 1892.

in Egypt. He employed Sálih Áqá to serve her, knowing that he was superbly qualified to undertake the responsibilities this entailed. Sálih Áqá had lived in the court of Ismá'íl Páshá, the viceroy of Egypt. He was accustomed to court life, therefore, and had mastered all of the manners and etiquette that pertained to the serving of a royal audience. He spoke excellent Arabic of the Egyptian dialect, and he was also fluent in Turkish of the Istanbuli dialect, which was the official language of the Ottoman Empire. He had been granted his freedom when the Egyptian dynasty ended, and he had eagerly accepted this opportunity.

After five months in Egypt, the Greatest Holy Leaf was prepared to return to Palestine. So pleased was she with Sálih Áqá's polite and modest composure, and his meticulous manners, that she thought him worthy to serve in the household of 'Abdu'l-Bahá. He accepted her invitation to return with her retinue. In 'Akká, he undertook to serve 'Abdu'l-Bahá.

In the trying days that followed Sálih Áqá's arrival in the Holy Land, the Covenant-breakers arose with shameless arrogance to challenge and oppose Him. They sent false and malicious reports to the Ottoman authorities claiming that 'Abdu'l-Bahá was preparing to raise the standard of revolt against the government. These enemies represented to the supersensitive Ottomans that 'Abdu'l-Bahá intended to make 'Akká and Haifa the new Mecca and Medina, that He had already raised the standard of rebellion in distant villages, that He had secretly raised an army of thirty thousand men. They declared that the real purpose of construction on the Shrine of the Báb was to provide a fortress and ammunition depot for that army on Mt. Carmel. And among their many other charges was the accusation that He had employed servants of the disbanded Egyptian court as His personal guard.

At this time, in 1896, my father and his brother were young men. They had plans to establish themselves in business in Cairo when they came to the Holy Land on pilgrimage. There they witnesed firsthand the story of Sálih Áqá. My father often told of how Sálih Áqá would don the colorful uniform of the royal court, with gilt buttons, scarlet trousers, and an Egyptian fez. In this impressive garb he would pace back and forth outside the house* of 'Abdu'l-Bahá in 'Akká, ready to welcome all guests. No doubt it was the sight of Sálih Áqá's imposing and dignified figure that engendered jealousy and malevolence in the hearts of the Covenant-breakers and gave rise to their defamatory report.

Every morning before sunrise, Sálih Áqá would open the doors to 'Abdu'l-Bahá's house and sprinkle water over the terraces. Regardless of whether or not 'Abdu'l-Bahá was at home, he insisted that the doors had to remain wide open to beckon the whole world to turn to Him. On one occasion, when the so-called Committee of Investigation was sent to 'Akká from Istanbul, there was great anxiety among the believers that the Master's safety might be in jeopardy. A number of friends gathered at the house of 'Abdu'l-Bahá to await His return for the midday meal.

By half past two, 'Abdu'l-Bahá had not yet returned, and this caused great concern among the

* This is the house known as the House of 'Abdu'lláh Páshá.

believers. A sandstorm was blowing outside, and a good deal of dust came sweeping into the hall where all were seated. One of the friends, becoming restless, rose to close the doors and lock out the wind and dust. Sálih Áqá, with composure interrupted him and exclaimed: "What kind of believer are you to close these doors, which are the refuge of the whole world, just because of a storm! If you are unable to bear a little discomfort for His sake, then it would be best for you to return to your home." The believer became deeply ashamed and returned to his place.

DESPITE THE FUTILITY of their efforts, 'Abdu'l-Bahá was heartbroken that the Covenant-breakers, who were members of His own family, would stoop to such levels of treachery and deceit. At another time, the friends were gathered in the reception room of the Master's house, and He was discussing the shameful machinations of those enemies. Suddenly Sálih Áqá entered the room. He paid his respects to the Master in the punctilious manner customary among Arabs and stood with his arms across his chest. 'Abdu'l-

Bahá knew that he sought permission to speak, and He invited him to do so.

Sálih Áqá then recounted a dream which he had had and wished to describe for the Master: "I dreamed I was standing outside the walls of the city of 'Akká, atop a hill overlooking the countryside. And I saw a legion of soldiers encamped on the plain between 'Akká and Haifa. As far as my eyes could see were soldiers and munitions. Their numbers were countless, like the waves of the sea. So densely were they garrisoned that the tethers of their tents had been knotted together. I was amazed, utterly astounded. I asked myself whose armies could be at war, and which side was this that could field so vast an army. Who, I asked myself, could be the commander of so mighty an army? I could see in the distance, from my vantage point, lanterns of gold reaching to the heavens above one magnificent tent.

"Suddenly you, 'Abdu'l-Bahá, summoned me to saddle your horse. When I did, you rose toward the camp. Passing beyond the town gates, you approached the tents, and I could see the soldiers line the avenues to greet you and salute you. It was as if they knew who you were. You, too, acknowledged their salutes. The respect with which they welcomed you and the manner of the homage they paid you served to heighten the enigma of the whole scene.

"As you arrived at the heart of the camp and that glorious tabernacle came into sight, you dismounted and continued to approach the tent with utmost veneration. I was now lost in bewilderment. Who, I thought, could be the commander of this army that he could invoke such respect from you? As you reached the drapes of the tent, the Commander appeared. Immediately I knew that it was Bahá'u'lláh. You fell at His feet and sought to prostrate yourself, but He prevented you. He embraced you, and together you entered the tent.

"I could, from my elevated position, see inside the tent as well. Battle plans and maps hung on the walls and covered the floor. It was as if you were conferring about strategy, and Bahá'u'lláh was advising. He was charging you with the command of that mighty army.

"Just then, I awoke."

All the while that Sálih Áqá was telling his

dream, tears streamed from the eyes of 'Abdu'l-Bahá. The friends too were in tears and appeared deeply moved. 'Abdu'l-Bahá asked him to step forward, embraced him, and kissed him on both eyes. He said: "O thou the radiance of whose glorious heart outshines the brilliance of thy polished skin! So pure is thy heart that it serves as the receptacle of the splendor of Bahá'u'lláh.

"The tabernacle of which thou didst dream is the sanctuary of the oneness of mankind, raised by the hand of the might of Bahá'u'lláh. Those maps and charts which thou didst see were plans for the guidance and edification of mankind which Bahá'u'lláh has entrusted to my hands. The Commander was none other than Bahá'u'lláh Himself, the Fashioner of the world. The legions of soldiers were the invisible hosts from on high who, by the mercy of Bahá'u'lláh, have come to render their assistance.

"The meaning of the dream is this: We shall be victorious over the Covenant-breakers and the other enemies of the Faith from within and without."

SÁLIH ÁQÁ

WHEN THE TIME CAME for my father and uncle to be dismissed from the presence of the Master, He summoned my father and told him that the service of Sálih Áqá had become a source of jealousy and envy on the part of the enemies of the Cause. He said: "Although I am unable to part with him, there are compelling reasons why he must not remain in 'Akká. Therefore, I want to designate him as your guardian, to escort and assist you. I want to remind you that you must extend the utmost respect and courtesy to him at all times."

My father fell at the feet of 'Abdu'l-Bahá, beseeching him and saying: "Whatever is your wish is my command. I shall unhesitatingly obey."

The following day, 'Abdu'l-Bahá summoned Sálih Áqá, my father, and my uncle. Addressing His servant, He said: "A friend has committed to my care something very precious which I must safeguard. I myself am unable to devote adequate time to the care required. I want to delegate the task to you. That which has been entrusted to me is the care of these two brothers. They are entering into commerce in a foreign land, and I want you to proceed to Cairo with them and to care for them as if they were your own sons."

Sálih Áqá could not hold back his tears. He implored the Master: "I know that you intend to drive me away from your gates. Had it been your wish to find a guardian for these two youth, with a single gesture of your hand you could have created a thousand."

'Abdu'l-Bahá consoled him. He explained that the brothers were planning to enter into business in Cairo and were not accustomed to the way of life in that land. "I wish for you to go with them on my behalf and be their tutor."

Sálih Áqá departed for Cairo with my father, my uncle, and Mírzá 'Ináyat Isfahání. There he lived for a few years until he passed away. The date of his death is uncertain.

INDEX

INDEX

INDEX

Made in the USA
Middletown, DE
21 February 2021